Hamlyn Gardening Guide

LAWN CARE

Arthur Hellyer

HAMLYN

Acknowledgements

Artwork by David Bryant

Colour photographs

John Cowley, p. 22; Flymo, p. 50 (top right and bottom); Arthur Hellyer, p. 60; David Johnson, p. 4; Murphy, p. 40 (top right and bottom left); Photos Horticultural, p. 26; The Harry Smith Horticultural Photographic Collection, p. 6, p. 40 (bottom right).
All other photographs by Hamlyn Publishing.

The editor would also like to acknowledge the help of Bob Andrews Ltd, Hayter plc, and Westwood.

First published under the title of *Your Lawn*
in 1970 by The Hamlyn Publishing Group Limited
This revised edition published in 1986
by Hamlyn Publishing,
Bridge House, London Road,
Twickenham, Middlesex, England

ISBN 0 600 30717 4

Filmset in 9½ pt on 11½ pt Palatino
by Wyvern Typesetting Limited, Bristol, England

Printed in Italy

CONTENTS

ESTABLISHING A LAWN – CHOICE OF MATERIAL

A good lawn adds greatly to the attractiveness of any garden and, thanks to the British climate, there is scarcely a garden in the country which could not have a good lawn provided it is made in the right way and looked after properly.

Four alternatives

There are four possible ways of making a lawn; by sowing seed, by laying cut turves, by planting tufts of creeping grass, or by simply mowing, weeding and tending the natural grass of the site. Each has its advantages and its drawbacks, but seeding is generally the best and cheapest method in the long run of producing a really fine lawn.

Lawns from seed

By using seed one can choose grasses specially suitable for the site and the purpose for which the lawn is required. Seedsman offer different lawn grasses or mixtures of grasses: some for fine lawns such as those used for bowling or putting greens, some a little coarser and harder wearing such as might be used for cricket pitches, golf fairways or football fields, and others suitable for shady or damp places where finer grasses would soon die out.

The drawbacks to seed are that the site must be specially well prepared to produce a reasonably fine and weed-free seed bed and that a few months must elapse before the lawn can be used to any extent.

A well-tended lawn provides a pleasing foil for many garden features and planting schemes. It can also create a welcome illusion of spaciousness

Turfing

Turf has the merit of quickness and certainty. Even on quite roughly prepared ground, turf will usually 'take' quite well and lawns made from turf can be used in a few weeks. But it is a relatively expensive method and unless one is buying very special turf such as that from sea-washed areas of Cumbria and elsewhere, which is used for the best bowling greens, it is generally quite impossible to find out precisely what grasses it contains – or, for that matter, what weeds. Turves commercially offered to new garden owners are very frequently cut from near-by building sites and are more likely to be composed of agricultural grasses than of those specially selected for garden use. Nevertheless, turf specially grown from seed is available from nurseries and is the best to buy.

Grass plants

Very beautiful lawns can also be made by planting tufts of creeping grass, but this is a comparatively slow method of lawn making as the tufts take some months to grow into one another and give a complete cover. Creeping grasses do not usually like very close mowing and are most suitable for purely ornamental lawns which can be a bit spongy.

Renovating existing grass

Finally there is the possibility of mowing down and weeding the existing grass on the site. This is the quickest and, at least in the short term, the cheapest method of all, and it has the additional merit that, since the grasses will be those that have survived on the site, they may be presumed to be well suited to it. They are not, however, very likely to be the best grasses for forming a fine lawn and they may contain some undesirable weeds that are hard to eradicate. So, in the long run, one may spend more money making natural grass into a good lawn than one would by digging it all in and starting again with selected seed.

Regular mowing and feeding of existing grass can achieve a good-looking sward.

INITIAL PREPARATION OF THE SITE

Unless one has decided to take a chance on renovating the native grass, digging is the very first job that must be done if one wants a good lawn. It need not be done with a spade, and on many soils it will certainly be easier to dig with a fork, but if the soil is light, sandy and dry it may slip through the prongs of the fork and then a spade will have to be used.

If there is a lot of ground to be prepared it may be better and it will certainly be less strenuous to prepare it mechanically. Small power-driven cultivators can be hired for self use or a contractor may be available who will come with his machine and do all the preparatory cultivation.

Removal of weeds

What is essential, whether fork, spade or cultivator is used, is that all the soil shall be well broken up to a depth of at least 23 cm (9 in), but 30 cm (12 in) is even better. It is also better if existing grass can be turned right in under the soil so that it rots. Many weeds will also decay in the same way if covered with several centimetres of soil, but some will survive and may sprout up again to become a nuisance unless they are either killed or carefully picked out. Couch grass, bindweed, docks, thistles and dandelions are all of this kind, and although some will gradually disappear with mowing others may remain to give permanent trouble.

There are two ways of dealing with this problem. Either all the larger and more persistent weeds, and particularly those with thick or creeping roots, are picked out and taken away as the work of soil preparation proceeds, or the whole site is treated with a herbicide a week or so before it is dug. A chemical named paraquat which is sold under the trade name Weedol is excellent for this purpose because it kills all grasses and most weeds and yet is non-persistent, so that it will do no damage to the grass that is subsequently grown on the site from seed, turves or tufts. It is purchased as crystals and, when made up with water according to manufacturers' instructions, can be applied direct to the grass and weeds from a watering can fitted with a fine rose or, better still, from a sprayer. In a few days the grass and weeds will start to wither and when all are brown they can be dug in with good expectation that most will not survive. Even after this treatment it is desirable to pick out large perennial roots such as those of dandelion, dock, thistle and bindweed. Glyphosate marketed as Tumbleweed and Roundup is more efficient in killing these perennial weeds but is much slower acting.

Drainage

Lawn grass needs moisture, but not an excess of it. A first-class lawn cannot be made on ground that is subject to periodic waterlogging. This can pose a problem on some very heavy clay soils, particularly in low-lying positions.

Very large lawns and sports fields can usually be provided with land drains and an outlet to a ditch or stream. This is seldom possible in a small garden, though it may be possible to dig a large and deep hole at the lowest point, fill it with stones, broken bricks or any other hard rubble, and then lead a drain from the lawn into it. If such a soakaway is deep enough to penetrate through the layer of clay or other subsoil that is holding up the water, the surplus water will percolate away, but if this is not possible the soakaway will just become a sump and, in wet weather, will soon overflow.

A fork is the easiest tool to use for clearing the ground. Turn the soil over to a depth of at least 23 cm (9 in).

Any weeds which remain should be removed at this time.

If a soakaway can be dug to allow water to percolate away freely it will provide the solution for periodic waterlogging of very heavy clay soils. A trench should be made to accommodate 8-cm (3-in) land drains set at a depth of 30 to 45 cm (12 to 18 in).

The land drains lead into a soakaway filled with stones, broken bricks or other hard rubble.

Soil is then replaced on top of the rubble to complete the soakaway.

Two other ways may be tried to overcome the problem of waterlogging and they may be used together or separately. One is to remove all the top soil to a depth of 15 to 20 cm (6 to 8 in), place a good layer of hard rubble all over the site and then replace the soil, if possible adding coarse sand and peat to it. The other possibility is to raise the lawn a few centimetres above the natural ground level. Either is likely to improve drainage and together they may solve the problem.

Naturally, this is something which must be considered at a very early stage. Many garden owners have made the mistake of making a lawn and only finding out the deficiencies of the soil drainage later, to their cost.

FINAL PREPARATION OF THE SITE

Careful preparation of the site is required whether the lawn is to be seeded, turfed or planted with tufts of creeping grass, but the greatest care in getting a very crumbly surface is necessary for seed sowing, since without this it will be impossible to get a reasonably even depth of sowing.

Choice of season

Lawns can be made at any time of year, but the two most favourable seasons for sowing grass seed are spring, from about mid-March to mid-April and late summer/early autumn from late August to the end of September. The soil is usually moist and warm then and these are the precise conditions required to ensure quick germination of the seed and strong growth of the seedlings. In winter the soil is cold and wet, germination is delayed and seed may rot or be picked up by birds before it has a chance to grow. In summer the soil is hot and dry and, even if showers enable the seed to germinate, a good deal of watering will almost certainly be required to keep the grass growing and prevent weeds getting the upper hand. All the same, in small gardens watering is not usually difficult to accomplish and summer sowing may be considered desirable if this means one will get a lawn sooner. Often spring sowing is most successful in the north and east of Britain, and autumn sowing in the south and west.

Digging should be completed as long as possible in advance of the sowing date – certainly a month ahead so that the soil has a chance to settle. Then a few days before the seed is actually sown the final preparation should take place.

The purpose of this is to break the rough clods of soil down to a fine, crumbly condition, to mix in a suitable quantity of grass food and to make the surface level. The tools required are a fork and rake and possibly also a spirit-level if a very true surface is required. But usually small- to medium-sized lawns can be levelled sufficiently accurately by eye, perhaps with a straight-edged plank placed this way and that over the surface as the work goes on to reveal any low or high places.

The use of fertilizers

But first, there is the matter of food. In this respect grass is little different from other plants and thrives on almost any of the manures and fertilizers which might be used to feed flowers, vegetables or fruits. It will grow well on soil fed with animal manure and stable manure well rotted with plenty of straw is specially good. Spent mushroom compost will improve soil texture but is not rich in plant food.

But the simplest solution for most gardeners is to buy ready-mixed fertilizer in a bag. There is no need to choose the most expensive kind; anything that is reasonably well balanced is suitable, and this simply means that it should contain about equal percentages of nitrogen, phosphoric acid (phosphates) and potash. These percentages will be shown on the bag, either with their full names as I have given them here, or reduced to chemical abbreviations – N for nitrogen, P_2O_5 for phosphoric acid and K_2O for potash.

Growmore fertilizer is widely available and well balanced, containing 7 per cent each of nitrogen, phosphoric acid and potash and it is often the best value for money. But in comparing price with price it is important to know that it is the actual percentage of each chemical that matters, e.g. a fertilizer with 14 per cent each of nitrogen, phosphoric acid and potash would be worth twice as much as Growmore since it would only have to be applied at half the rate in order to produce the same result.

Peat is excellent for improving the texture of the soil. However, baled peat is too dry for use as it is packed, and water must be poured into the bales and allowed to soak in before the peat is applied.

The correct rate for a Growmore-type mixture would be 128 g per m^2 (4 oz per sq yd). A handful of fertilizer is usually about 60 g (2 oz) so on this basis two handfuls would be required for each square metre of ground. A good stride is approximately a metre, so by walking down the length of the lawn site, taking good long steps and counting them as one goes, and doing the same for the width and then multiplying one figure by the other, the approximate number of square metres to be treated can be calculated.

A topdressing of fertilizer being applied to the lawn site.

Topdressings of peat and fertilizer can be worked in with a Canterbury hoe or fork.

Improving soil texture

Unless the soil is of a medium texture it will almost certainly be improved by the addition of some peat as well. This will make sticky clay soils less inclined to clog, it will prevent open, sandy soils from drying out too quickly and it will improve the quality of chalky soils. About 1 kg per m^2 (2 lb per sq yd) of granulated peat will be sufficient in most cases, though if the soil is very extreme in character, i.e. very heavy, very light or very chalky, the quantity could usefully be doubled. No harm can be done with an excess of peat, but harm can be done by using too much fertilizer, so weigh the latter carefully, bearing in mind that the stronger it is, i.e. the higher the analysis figures on the bag, the less one will need. Usually, however, the manufacturers print a recommended rate of application.

The best time to apply both peat and fertilizer is immediately before the rough clods left by digging are broken down to a seed bed. Then, as the plot is forked and raked, the chemicals and peat will be thoroughly mixed with the top 5 cm (2 in) of soil which is where they are needed.

Both peat and fertilizer should be scattered as evenly as possible over the surface. It may be wise to divide each into two equal parts, one part to be scattered while walking up and down the plot lengthwise, the other while moving to and fro across its breadth. It is worth taking pains about this, particularly with the fertilizer, for uneven distribu-

After rough levelling the whole area should be trodden over, by shuffling backwards and forwards across the site systematically.

tion will result in uneven growth of grass which will look unsightly and take time to rectify.

When these topdressings, of whatever nature they may be, have been spread, work over the plot with a fork, using it mainly with swinging blows to break up the clods rather than to turn them over and possibly bring weeds back to the surface. Some gardeners may prefer to use a tool known as a Canterbury hoe, which has three or four fork-like prongs attached at right angles to a long handle. This is used like a rake and its longer prongs are excellent for breaking up hard clods of soil. An illustration showing one of these hoes in use is shown on page 13.

After a lapse of at least one day, to allow the soil to settle further, give the soil a final raking. The soil level should also be adjusted at this time.

A long straight-edged plank held on its narrow edge is useful at this stage, a spirit-level also being used if absolute accuracy is required.

Levelling and firming

As the work of breaking down continues a first rough levelling up can also be given, soil being thrown from obviously high spots into those that are clearly low.

After this first knocking down the whole area should be trodden, partly to assist in breaking any remaining lumps of soil but even more to ensure that there are no loose places which would settle later and cause hollows in the lawn. The right way to tread is to shuffle backwards and forwards across the lawn, covering every centimetre of it, and again it is wise to do this twice, first working the length of the lawn and then across its breadth.

Final preparation

If time permits, let at least one day elapse between this first breaking down and the final raking. This will give the surface a chance to dry out a little and so make raking easier and more effective.

Any type of rake can be used for the final preparation but a fairly large, steel-pronged rake is the most convenient. Start at one end of the plot and work backwards to the other end. Use the rake with pushing as well as pulling actions and make every attempt to break up remaining lumps of soil rather than to remove them. Only surface stones and debris must be raked right off the site. The stones may well prove useful for making the foundations of a garden path.

The final levelling should be carried out as this raking proceeds, soil being drawn or pushed from high places to those that are low. A surprising degree of accuracy can be achieved with the use of the eye alone but more precise levelling may be felt necessary. A long straight-edged plank held on its narrow edge is useful for this task, and if it is really essential that the lawn be absolutely level, a spirit level may be placed on the upper edge of the plank to check this over the area of the site.

SEEDING AND INITIAL LAWN CARE

There are many different kinds of grass and at least a score which might be used in lawn making, but it is not necessary to have any detailed knowledge of them since most seedsmen offer mixtures blended for special purposes, and only a few offer seed of individual varieties or state precisely what grasses they put in their mixtures.

The mixtures fall broadly into three main groups; mixtures of fine grasses, usually fescues and agrostis species (bents) of which one named Browntop (*Argostis tenuis*) is the favourite; coarser mixtures including perennial rye-grasses; and mixtures for shady places – the most difficult for grasses to cope with – which are likely to include Rough-stalked Meadow Grass and possibly Crested Dog's-tail.

Seed of the best fescues and bents is considerably more expensive than that of rye-grass and meadow grasses, usually takes longer to germinate and the grass is slower growing. However, fescues and bents stand close cutting well, which rye and meadow grasses do not. It is mixtures of this kind that should be chosen for all lawns that are to be kept regularly close mown, but for grass that is simply to be an ornamental setting for trees and shrubs and is to be cut with a rotary mower, selected varieties of rye-grass or Smooth-stalked Meadow Grass may be more suitable being stronger, harder wearing and requiring less maintenance. Named varieties of rye grasses such as Hunter and Elka make a much denser firm-textured turf than will perennial rye grass and can be cut shorter without injury, Elka to as little as 1 cm ($\frac{3}{4}$ in). They can be used alone or in mixtures.

Rates of sowing

The usual recommended rate of sowing is 64 g per m^2 (2 oz per sq yd). This gives a quick coverage of grass, but can be costly if fine grasses are to be used on a fairly large area. Provided the soil has been well prepared, weeds have been

Seeding

Mark out the plot in metre squares. Then measure the seed for one square in a plastic cup and mark the level. This is a simple way of ensuring accurate sowing.

Alternatively, mark off the plot with string in metre-wide strips, divide the seed into portions sufficient for each and sow accordingly. However, this is a rather less accurate method.

Grass seed has been sown evenly over the area and is being raked in. Before sowing the soil should have been raked over in one direction to make tiny parallel furrows. These are now raked over at right angles to ensure even coverage.

An easy method of seed sowing is to use a wheeled fertilizer distributor. The only technicality is the setting of the roller to give the correct rate of application.

removed and one is willing to wait a little and nurse the young grass along for a few months, sowing rates as low as 32 g per m^2 (1 oz per sq yd) can be quite satisfactory. A handful of lawn seed is approximately 25 g (1 oz).

Methods of sowing

Immediately before sowing rake the whole surface once more, but in one direction only so that the rake marks are all parallel to one another like tiny furrows. Then scatter the seed evenly over the surface and rake again, but this time at right angles to the former raking. This will close the furrows and cover most of the seed.

There are many different ways of sowing grass seed. One can just walk up and down the plot, scattering the seed by hand until it is all distributed, but unless one has experience it is difficult to get even distribution this way.

An alternative is to mark out the whole plot with string in metre-wide strips, divide the seed into equal portions, one for each strip, and sow each separately. For the beginner this is likely to result in a far better job.

Alternatively one can carry the whole thing a stage further. Have two lots of strings, lengthwise and crosswise, so that the plot is marked out in square metres; find a measure that will hold just 60 g (2 oz) of seed – or 25 g (1 oz) if the lower seeding rate is to be adopted – and scatter one measure of seed over each square. This is the most accurate way of all and is to be recommended where expensive seed is being used at rather a low rate of seeding.

But the easiest way is to use a wheeled fertilizer distributor, for this will distribute seed just as accurately and as quickly as it will distribute chemicals. The only difficulty may be to find the right setting to ensure that the correct amount of seed is sown. One way is to run the machine filled with seed over a sheet of paper in just the same way as I have shown in the pictures on page 27 where the adjustment is being made for fertilizer application. Measure the width of the distributing part of the machine and then mark on the paper a sufficient length to give half a square metre at this width, i.e. if the machine is half a metre wide it will be necessary to run it one metre on the paper to cover half a square metre. Now choose a setting that seems right, run the machine twice from mark to mark, carefully pick up the paper and tip the seed into a scale or measuring cup. It will be easy to see if there is too much or too little seed and to adjust the setting until it is just right for sowing at the correct rate.

Care of the new lawn

Bird control

Most grass seed is pre-treated by the seedsmen with an effective bird deterrent. However, this will not stop birds taking dust baths, nor cats scratching. Sometimes the deterrent mixture is provided with the

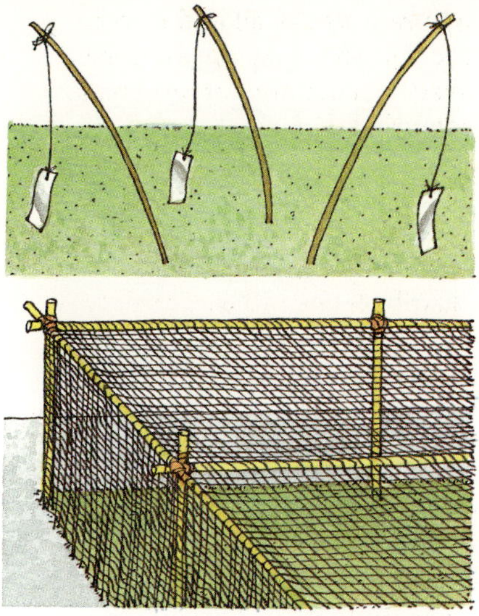

Protect your newly-sown lawn with paper streamers tied on canes. Alternatively, use fine-mesh plastic netting (or chicken wire) supported clear of the soil. This should keep cats at bay and prevent birds having dust baths.

seed for mixing by the gardener. But untreated seed must be protected with bird scarers or black cotton stretched a few centimetres above soil level between pieces of cane or stick, or by one of the methods shown in the illustrations above.

Watering

If the weather after sowing is very dry it may be necessary to water, but it is better if this can be avoided as watering at this time tends to compact the surface and so hinder the germination of the seed.

Mowing

Grass seedlings should appear in anything from eight days to a month after sowing, according to the conditions and the type of seed used. Rye-grass and meadow grass germinate most rapidly, and in damp warm weather will grow quicker than when it is cold and dry.

A lawn grown from seed should be cut for the first time when the grass is 4 to 5 cm ($1\frac{1}{2}$ to 2 in) high. It is essential to use a very sharp-bladed mower for this first mowing, otherwise the seedlings may be dragged out of the soil. If a light roller is available it may be used with advantage a day or so before the lawn is cut, but the surface must be no more than moist. If it is wet, the soil will be compacted and growth will be checked with the result that some grass may be killed.

If the area involved is small the grass can be given its first cutting with a pair of hand shears, but these must also be sharp to avoid tearing the grasses.

Weed control

However carefully the site has been prepared, there will probably be some weeds among the grass. Many of the most common, such as Groundsel, Chickweed and Shepherd's Purse, will not survive a few mowings, but others may prove more persistent and will have to be removed by hand, either by pulling out the shallow rooting kinds or digging out the deeper rooted kinds with a spade or narrow bladed trowel.

On pages 35 and 36 are pictures of eight commonly encountered lawn weeds which it would be useful to learn to identify.

TURFING AND OTHER METHODS

The preparation of a lawn site for turf is the same as for seed. The best season for laying turf is autumn, from mid-September until the end of October, but turf can be laid at any time of the year provided it is well looked after. In winter it may be very slow to establish itself and in summer it may succumb to drought unless it is well watered in dry weather.

Turves are commonly cut in rectangular strips 1 m by 30 cm (3 ft by 1 ft; and about 4 cm ($1\frac{1}{2}$ in) thick if from meadows, but often only 1 cm

A half-moon edging knife is used to cut around the turf with a garden line and a 1-m (3-ft) wooden strip to act as guides to the correct dimensions.

A turfing iron is inserted under a cut strip and the turf is lifted. An ordinary garden spade is a good substitute if a turfing iron is unavailable.

($\frac{1}{2}$ in) thick from specially-seeded nursery grass. These are rolled up, rather like a Swiss roll, for ease of handling and delivery and this can be a disadvantage since some of the soil may break away from the turves during the rolling and unrolling. This is why the very best quality turves are usually cut in 30 cm (12 in) squares which can be handled flat, but these are not always easy to obtain and they usually cost more for the area covered.

If the turves have been well cut they will all be of identical thickness and can be laid without further preparation, but if they are uneven in thickness it will save time to make a shallow wooden trough with inside measurements exactly those of the turf, and 4 cm ($1\frac{1}{2}$ in) deep. The turves are placed grass side downwards in this trough and a carving knife or scythe blade is drawn across them, so that it cuts off any surplus thickness. However, this should be unnecessary with special nursery turf.

Turves should be relaid as quickly as possible after they are delivered. If there is an inevitable delay because of bad weather or lack of time, they should be unrolled and laid out grass side upwards in any convenient place. They should not be stacked one on top of the other as this will cause the grass to go yellow and eventually die.

Turves are laid in straight rows, usually starting at one end or side of the plot, but the turves in alternate rows are staggered so that although the joints between the turves form continuous lines in one

The turf is then rolled, care being taken not to let too much soil break away from the underside of the turf during the operation.

When the thickness of the turf is not even, place it in an easily-made shallow trough grass side downwards and pare off any surplus soil with an old scythe blade or carving knife.

When making a new lawn from turf the ground must first be thoroughly prepared as described earlier in this book. Always stand on a plank to protect the newly-laid turves and rake the soil frequently.

Lay the turves in staggered rows (like a brick wall), butted tightly against each other. Then firm each one down well with your hands.

Make sure that the turves are in close contact with the soil, by lightly beating them with the back of a spade.

Fill in the cracks between the newly-laid turves with fine soil and work this in with the back of a rake or use a brush.

direction, they make broken lines, like bricks in a wall, in the other direction. This helps to bind the turves together and makes it less likely that they will move during the few weeks it takes them to root down into the soil.

If the lawn has no straight edge it will be easiest to lay the first line of turves a little inside one of the edges, using a line stretched between two pegs to get the row absolutely straight. Then work can proceed both away from the edge and towards it, the outside turves being trimmed to shape with a knife or lawn-edging tool after they have been laid. The soil may be frequently raked as work proceeds to eliminate footprints and keep a perfectly level surface. If, when laid, any turf appears to be higher or lower than its neighbour, this should be adjusted at once by removing or adding a little soil under it. The turves may be lightly beaten down with the back of a spade or a wooden lawn beater to ensure that they make close contact with the soil but heavy beating will cause more harm than good.

When all the turves have been laid, a light topdressing of fine granulated peat, or a mixture of peat and sharp sand, may be scattered all over and then brushed this way and that so that it fills up any remaining small spaces.

The grass on a turfed lawn can be cut as soon as it has grown sufficiently to need this. In a very few weeks it should have rooted down into the soil so that the turves are firmly anchored.

Using grass plants

Lawns from planted tufts are best made in spring or autumn when conditions are most favourable for rapid growth. The grass used is generally creeping bent (*Agrostis stolonifera*), but there are many different forms of this, some with very fine leaves, others much coarser. It is the fine-leaved ones that should be used for lawn making.

Large plants are pulled to pieces and then several of those with leaves and roots attached are bunched together to form a tuft with the roots all at one end, and this is then planted with a trowel. If spaced about 23 cm (9 in) apart each way the tufts will cover the ground fairly quickly and can be mown directly they have formed a

When making a lawn of creeping grass several small pieces are bunched together to form a tuft, and this is planted with a trowel. If spaced about 23 cm (9 in) apart each way these tufts will cover the ground quite quickly.

continuous sward. However, this grass makes a lot of its roots on the surface and so must not be mown too closely or the roots will be exposed and the plants may die.

Using the native turf

To form a lawn from the native turf of the site is mainly a matter of management, i.e. regular cutting, feeding and weeding to improve its quality. All the same, if the surface is irregular it may be necessary to do some levelling before the process of improvement commences. To do this the turf in the high or low places should always be cut and lifted, soil then being removed or added as necessary, after which the turves are replaced. The alternative, to spread soil on top of the hollows and to beat or roll down the humps, will only result in dead patches, poor growth and disappointment. Turves can be cut with either a spade or a lawn-

A carefully tended lawn like this immaculate sward shown, provides a magnificent background for decorative plant displays, trees and shrubs.

edging knife and lifted with either a spade or a special turf-lifting tool.

Bravura turf

A third alternative is to buy Bravura turf which is specially grown from seed in a 1-cm ($\frac{3}{4}$-in) thick layer of special compost spread over a thin polythene sheet laminated to a fine mesh net. This gives the turf great strength and allows it to be rolled up in 75-cm by 3.2-m ($2\frac{1}{2}$- by 11-ft) sections. The polythene sheet is stripped off before the turf is relaid and the grass quickly roots down into the soil.

When a lawn is being made from native turf, any irregularities in the surface can be corrected by lifting small areas and adding (or taking away) soil. A half-moon edging knife is being used here to cut the turves.

Levelling the new soil with a rake. Any stones or other unwanted material are removed at this time.

Relaying the turves after the soil has been levelled. As when laying purchased turves, they should be beaten down lightly with the back of a spade so that they make close contact with the soil.

FEEDING AND WATERING THE LAWN

To be maintained in good condition lawns must be reguarly fed, watered in dry weather, properly mown practically throughout the year, kept free of weeds, pests and diseases and be occasionally rolled, raked and slit or perforated to remove accumulations of dead plants and to let in air. A great many lawn owners carry out only the mowing and then wonder why their lawns do not look very good.

Grass that is starved becomes weak and yellowish and is very easily infested with weeds and moss which may eventually take the place of the grass. Since grass

A fertilizer distributor is a great convenience but it is important that the setting should be right.

To test the flow, run the machine after setting over a measured strip of paper (note tape measure beside paper).

takes quite a lot out of the soil it should be fed at least once a year if its quality is to be maintained. The best time for such a single feeding is spring, but even better results will be produced by feeding three times each year, in spring, early summer and early autumn.

The use of fertilizers

For the spring and early summer feeding a well-balanced fertilizer is required, as in the preparation of soil for lawns (see page 12).

Rates of application

The rate of application will depend upon the strength of the fertilizer but anything with analysis around 7 per cent nitrogen, 7 per cent phosphoric acid and 7 per cent potash may be used at 96 g per m^2 (3 oz per sq yd) in March or April with a second application at 64 g per m^2 (2 oz per sq yd) in June. However, always look for the manufacturers' instructions and follow them to the letter, for an overdose of fertilizer can scorch and even kill the grass. It is more likely to do so in hot, dry weather than when it is cool and damp, hence the recommendation of a lower rate of application in June.

For the early autumn (September) application, something quite different is required, as any fertilizer with this percentage of nitrogen would encourage disease in winter. What is needed then is a fertilizer with about 2 per cent nitrogen, 10 to 12 per cent phosphoric acid and 6 per cent or more potash. Such autumn lawn dressings are prepared by the chemical fertilizer manufacturers and should be used at about 64 g per m^2 (2 oz per sq yd) unless otherwise stated.

Since over application of fertilizer can be so very damaging it is important to ensure that the correct quantity is spread evenly all over the lawn. What was said about the application of fertilizer in soil preparation (see page 12) applies with even greater force since the chemicals are going to be scattered on top of the growing grass. If the mixture is to be spread by hand it will be wise to mark out the area in metre-wide strips, weigh or measure the correct amount of fertilizer for each and scatter it strip by strip. If a fertilizer distributor is used care should be taken to get the right setting by running it over a marked paper (see page 27).

Care must also be taken that when pushing the spreader up and down the lawn, the whole area is covered without overlap. Some machines are fitted with marking devices which show clearly where they have been. If they are not it may again be wise to mark the strips or to apply the fertilizer when there is still dew on the grass and the tracks of the wheels can be seen clearly.

When turning or when starting to move, some machines deliver an extra quantity of fertilizer unless shut off momentarily. It is easy to get brown patches at each end of the lawn by neglecting this simple precaution.

The application of water

Watering is the counterpart of feeding, since grass, like other plants, takes in all its food from the soil in solution. Without water, grass cannot feed, however much fertilizer or manure has been put into the soil.

For long periods in the British Isles the rainfall is sufficient, but every year there are periods, sometimes lasting several months, when extra water is required to keep grass in good condition. There are all kinds of ways in which it can be applied, but the best are those that spread the water evenly and rather slowly so that it has time to sink in and does not run off the surface. Oscillating sprinklers have the merit of covering rectangular, not circular, areas with water, and so on large lawns they can be moved on without either overlapping or missing any places. Rotating sprinklers are simple and rarely give any trouble and pulsating (or impulse) sprinklers can throw water a long way and be adjusted to cover a full circle or any arc of a circle on a large lawn. Pop-up sprinklers are placed permanently just below turf level and are pushed up by the pressure of water when this is turned on. There are numerous other devices and you should visit your local garden centre or sundriesman for ideas.

Do not delay watering until the grass is beginning to go brown. As soon as the soil in the surrounding beds is obviously dry, give the lawn a good soaking and repeat every day until there is an appreciable rainfall. The most common fault is to have sprinklers spraying for too short a time so that only the surface is moistened.

An oscillating sprinkler which waters a rectangular area. It can be adjusted to give a full sweep, to cover one side only or a central area.

MOWERS AND MOWING

Mowing is the most important operation of all since the way it is done will very largely determine the kind of grass that predominates in the lawn. The coarser grasses, such as rye-grass and the meadow grasses, cannot stand very close mowing and will gradually die out if cut too hard. The fine fescues and bents, by contrast, thrive on fairly close mowing, but even they can be killed by setting the blades too low, particularly in hot, dry weather.

Height of cut

If a lawn of rye-grass or meadow grass is being made, the blades of the mower should never be set closer than 2 cm (¾ in) to the soil, and they can even be set as high as 4 cm (1½ in). A lawn made from a fine grass mixture may be mown as close as 0.5 cm (¼ in) though rather more, say ¾ to 1 cm (⅜ to ½ in) will be adequate for ordinary home use.

Close mowing is nearly always done with a cylinder type mower, rotaries being on the whole more suitable for lawns left with 1 cm (½ in) or more grass. The finished effect of mowing with the cylinder machine depends partly on the blades being kept sharp and properly adjusted, so that the revolving blades make close contact throughout their length with the fixed bottom blade, but it is also affected by the number of cuts per metre of forward movement. This is a characteristic of the machine, depending on its gearing and the number of blades on the revolving cylinder or reel. Rough-cut machines may give no more than 25 cuts per metre, whereas the very finest cutting machines may give 130 cuts per metre. A fair average for home use is about 35 to 45 cuts per metre, for a hand-pushed machine and 70 to 80 for a power-driven machine. The more cuts per metre given, the more power will be needed to propel the machine and the more likely it is to jam if the grass is long or wet. A large number of cuts gives a smoother, less ribbed finish and, like close cutting, tends to encourage the growth of finer grasses.

The more closely and finely a lawn is cut the more frequently the work will have to be done. Fine lawns cut to $\frac{3}{4}$cm ($\frac{3}{8}$in) with a mower giving 100 cuts per metre will need mowing at least twice and possibly three times a week in late spring and early summer, and even in winter may need an occasional cut when the surface is not too wet.

At the other extreme, the Continental or American style lawn, mown to about 2.5 to 4 cm (1 to $1\frac{1}{2}$ in) with a rotary machine, will only need one cut a week even at the height of its growth and can usually be left uncut from the end of October until early March. Such lawns have a very good appearance when grown as a setting for trees and shrubs but are useless for any kind of ball game.

I have described the different types of mower, both hand-propelled and powered, between pages 49 and 54, and there are illustrations showing various models and their design features.

Setting the lawn mower

To check the height of cut with a cylinder mower, turn the machine on its side, place a straight edge between the front and rear rollers (or one side wheel and rear rollers of a side-wheel-drive machine) and measure the distance between the straight edge and the cutting edge of the bottom blade. With a rotary machine lay the straight edge diagonally across from a front to a back wheel and measure from it to one of the blades turned directly in line with it. The height of cut of air-cushion rotaries can only be checked by experiment on the lawn.

Adjusting the height of the front roller on a cylinder-type mower, which determines the height at which the grass is cut.

When correctly adjusted the blades should cut cleanly a strip of paper when this is placed between them and the bottom plate.

WEED CONTROL

Weed eradication has been enormously simplified by the introduction of selective weedkillers. There are now a number of these chemicals and they are sold under various trade names. None kills every kind of weed that may grow in grass and only a few kill clover, but each has its own uses and between them they can destroy about 90 per cent of the weeds commonly encountered in turf. As with so much else in gardening, a great deal of time and trouble can be saved by early and regular attention to weed control.

Application of weedkillers

The term 'selective' is applied to weedkillers which will kill some plants but not others. Those used on lawns do not kill the grass, though they may check its growth for a few days. However, they do kill a great many other plants, not only lawn weeds but garden plants which may be growing in the beds or borders around the lawn. So when using these weedkillers it is very important to apply them only to the lawn and not to allow them to splash, trickle or drift on to surrounding plants. Nor should too great a quantity be given lest it soaks down and reaches the roots of trees or shrubs growing beneath the turf. All that is necessary is to wet the leaves of the weeds and this can be done quickly and efficiently by fitting an ordinary watering can with a sprinkle bar, which can be purchased from any garden centre. The surface of the weeds should be lightly wetted holding the bar only a centimetre or so above the turf and walking up and down the lawn so that every centimetre is covered.

The manufacturers' instructions should be read carefully before using selective weedkillers to ensure that over-strong mixtures are not applied to the grass.

Time of application

Selective weedkillers may be used at any time from spring until

This useful appliance is fitted onto your garden hose and mixes as it sprays. The adjustable metering device ensures the weed-killer is correctly diluted and the deflector keeps drift to an absolute minimum.

autumn, but are most effective when growth is rapid, which is usually in late spring and early summer. It is a good policy to apply weedkiller a few days after the early summer feed. The fertilizer will have the effect of stimulating the growth of the weeds, making them more susceptible to the weedkiller. At the same time the fertilizer will help the grass to make a quick recovery from the slight check which the application of selective weedkiller will cause.

The use of lawn sand

An older method of killing weeds chemically is by the use of lawn sand and this still has its uses since it will kill some weeds which resist

Spot treatment is another method of weed control. Painting a weedkiller directly onto the leaves from the container ensures no spillage.

Applying lawn sand to a small group of weeds. After a day or so these will be scorched out.

all the selective weedkillers. Lawn sand is a mixture of sulphate of ammonia and sulphate of iron and is purchased as a fine powder ready for use. It is sprinkled lightly on the weeds, or weedy patches, and in a day or so it scorches them out. It may scorch the grass too, but provided no overdose has been given, this will recover in a week or so and grow all the more strongly since both the chemical ingredients of lawn sand are fertilizers.

The best time for using lawn sand is when the weather is dry and likely to remain so for a few days. Its effectiveness depends very largely on it remaining for some time on the fairly broad flat leaves of the lawn weeds, and any rain coming quickly after it has been spread may wash it off.

Eliminating coarse grasses

Neither selective weedkillers nor lawn sand will kill the coarse grasses which may infest lawns and spoil their appearance, and the only ways of dealing with these are either to cut them out, plant by plant, or to lift the bad areas of turf and re-seed or re-turf.

Moss control

Moss is not killed by selective lawn weedkillers but it is sensitive to ordinary lawn sand or to sulphate of iron on its own dissolved in water at 3 g per litre ($\frac{1}{2}$ oz per gallon) and applied from a watering can fitted with a sprinkler bar. There are also numerous proprietary mosskillers for use on lawns and these should be used according to manufacturers' instructions. However, development of moss is a sure sign that something is wrong. It could be build-up of debris, soil compaction, close mowing 'scalping' the surface or deep shade. Without rectifying the root cause the moss will always return (see pages 42 to 45 for advice on maintenance).

Ground thistle (*Carduus acaulis*)

Plantain (*Plantago media*)

Buttercup, daisy, dandelion and plantain

Selfheal (*Prunella vulgaris*)

Cranesbill (*Geranium molle*)

Thyme-leaved speedwell (*Veronica serphyllifolia*)

Moss

Yarrow (*Achillea millefolium*)

PESTS AND DISEASES

Grass suffers from various pests and diseases just like any other plant, but these are not likely to prove very troublesome under ordinary domestic conditions.

Pests

Leatherjackets

The pest most likely to give trouble is the leatherjacket. This is a large grub, superficially shaped like a caterpillar but without legs, very sluggish in its movements and with very tough grey skin, hence its popular name. It is the larva of the daddy-long-legs or crane fly, and it lives in the soil feeding on the roots of grass and other plants.

A few leatherjackets will usually be found in any grass that is turned over and in small numbers may do little visible harm to the turf. But if they become numerous the grass dies, usually in small patches at first, but spreading if the infestation is heavy. The damage is similar in appearance to that caused by some turf diseases, by careless use of fertilizers or by a bitch wetting the grass. It is most likely to appear in summer and may be most severe in dry weather when loss of some roots puts a severe strain on the grass. However, a simple test will usually determine whether the dead patches are the result of leatherjacket damage. Soak a badly damaged area thoroughly with water until the soil is really saturated and then lay a wet sack or a polythene sheet (a large polythene fertilizer bag split open will do well) over it. The excess water drives the air out of the soil and the covering prevents any more air getting into it. As a result any leatherjackets are driven to the surface and a few hours later will be found lying there. If this test shows that leatherjackets are the cause of the trouble the lawn should be watered with a good insecticide such as diazinon or carbaryl.

Earthworms

Earthworms are not exactly a lawn pest, indeed in moderate numbers they do more good than harm since they aerate the turf and draw dead leaves and other debris into the soil. But earthworms make casts of soil on the surface which in wet weather become sticky and when trodden on or run over by a mower or roller spread out and smother small areas of grass. In moderate numbers this can be dealt with by brushing with a besom or broom or by whisking with a long flexible bamboo cane to break up and distribute the casts. But earthworms in excess can be a great nuisance and steps must be taken to reduce their numbers.

There are two effective remedies, Mowrah Meal and chlordane. Mowrah Meal should be purchased as a fine powder which is spread over the surface at about 256 g per m^2 ($\frac{1}{2}$ lb per sq yd) and must be well watered in. The worms come to the surface to die and must then be swept up. Chlordane has the advantage that less water is required and the worms die in the soil. It is purchased as a liquid for dilution with water and is applied from a watering can fitted with a sprinkle bar or fine rose. The most effective periods for de-worming lawns are in spring or early autumn when the weather is mild and the soil moist.

Cutworms and wireworms
Various soil caterpillars, known collectively as cutworms, occasionally damage turf in the same way as leatherjackets and so do the grubs of chafer beetles, including the familiar cockchafer or May bug. Wireworms too, may be troublesome especially on newly-sown lawns. These are the larvae of click beetles, are 1 to 2.5 cm ($\frac{1}{2}$ to 1 in) long, thin, with hard, shiny yellow-orange skins. Like all these other soil pests they live on the roots of grasses and other plants. Measures taken to eliminate leatherjackets will also kill these soil pests and

To find out if leatherjackets are present soak the damaged area thoroughly with water until the soil is saturated.

Then cover this soaked area with a wet sack or polythene sheet to exclude the air. The grubs will then be forced to the surface.

chlordane applied against earthworms will also account for many of them. It might seem a wise general precaution therefore, on high quality lawns to apply chlordane as part of the regular maintenance programme once a year in March or April.

Moles

Moles live on earthworms, wireworms and other small creatures in the soil and would be most useful to the gardener if they did not tunnel all over the place, throwing up the excavated soil in mounds and causing the surface to collapse. All this can be disastrous on a lawn from which moles must be rigidly excluded. Moles can be destroyed or driven out by placing special smoke bombs in their runs, and they can be trapped in steel mole traps set across the runs. Gloves should be worn when setting traps as moles have a highly developed sense of smell. When the trap has been set in place, pieces of turf should be placed over it to exclude light from the run.

Inspect the trap regularly and if a mole has been captured take it to some local area of woodland or rough meadow and let it go.

Leatherjackets, the larvae of the daddy-long-legs or crane fly, can be injurious to grass if present in large numbers. They are most likely to appear in summer.

Ants

Occasionally ants become a nuisance by nesting on lawns and throwing up ant-hills. Highly effective ant-baits can be purchased which, if placed where the ants are seen will quickly destroy them.

Diseases

Experts distinguish a number of diseases of grass all caused by fungi of one kind or another, but the ordinary gardener need only be concerned with determining whether damage is in fact due to a fungus or to some other cause, since this will be sufficient to determine the treatment which should be given.

Many turf diseases are most troublesome between autumn and spring. They thrive in cold, damp conditions and where an excess of nitrogenous fertilizer has been applied too late in the summer, causing soft, disease-prone growth. Sometimes the fungus can be detected as fine white or pink threads on the dying grass and in wet weather fungus-infected grass tends to become slimy. It first becomes yellow, then brown, and affected patches may be small and more or less circular, or much larger and less regular. In summer it may be hard to distinguish these symptoms from those caused by leatherjackets and other soil pests, but if the damage worsens in autumn it is fairly certain that disease is the cause.

Treatment is very largely a matter of improving lawn care, feeding correctly, aerating and gathering and removing lawn trimmings. Chemicals may also be used to kill the fungi, the most effective for general use in private gardens being benomyl, calomel (mercurous chloride) and thiophanate-methyl. All these are available in proprietary formulations, calomel usually prepared for club-root control in brassica crops but equally suitable for use on lawns. If the formulation is a dust it should be sprinkled on the grass, if a liquid it should be diluted with water according to the manufacturers' instructions and applied from a watering can fitted with a fine rose or sprinkle bar.

Earthworms are only a pest in the sense that they make casts of soil which are unsightly and when trodden on in wet weather or spread by the mower or roller, can smother small areas of grass.

Wireworms, the larvae of click beetles, may be troublesome, especially on newly-sown lawns. They live on the roots of grasses and other plants.

The trade mark of the mole, an industrious little creature whose presence is a nuisance under a lawn.

Fairy rings are caused by various capped fungi. Apart from digging up the lawn and sterilizing the soil, little else can be done.

GENERAL MAINTENANCE

Grass grows best in reasonably firm soil, the fine grasses being more sensitive to this than the coarser kinds such as rye-grass and meadow grass. The object of treading the soil before sowing seed or laying turf is to provide this firmness, and established lawns are rolled to maintain it. But if the soil is already sufficiently firm there is no point in rolling, and it may actually do harm by compacting the soil too much and so excluding air and water.

Rolling

Turf used for ball games requiring great accuracy, e.g. croquet lawns, bowling and putting greens and cricket pitches, must be rolled frequently and fairly heavily to maintain a true playing surface, but when the playing season is over they have to be perforated and slit and dressed with grit and peat to undo the harmful compaction that the constant rolling has done to the turf.

The point of all this is that private gardeners, observing what is done by professional greenkeepers, often tend to follow their lead blindly without stopping to enquire whether it is really necessary, or even desirable, on the home lawn. The answer is that unless the lawn is used for ball games requiring a perfectly true surface, repeated and heavy rolling is certainly not desirable. For lawns used solely for ornament and left with a centimetre or more of grass it is unlikely that any rolling would be required.

Fine lawns cut with a roller mower will get most of the rolling they require as they are cut, but if they get to feel too springy, a light roller may be used on them. One weighing about 100 kg (2 cwt) will do well.

Rolling should never be used to correct a really bumpy lawn since all it will do is make the ground too hard in the high places and so produce uneven growth and poor turf.

Rolling should never be done when the turf is very wet or very dry. It needs to be just nicely moist so that it yields to the roller without becoming pasted down.

It should seldom be necessary to roll a home lawn more than once a fortnight in spring and summer and not at all in autumn or winter.

Removing the debris

Raking and brushing are necessary to get rid of the debris of dead or decaying material which inevitably collects in turf. If left to accumulate this can, in time build up to a sufficient thickness to absorb much rain and prevent it reaching the grass roots below. For this condition at its most extreme, greenkeepers have invented the expressive term 'thatch' and have developed special power-driven rakes to cut it up and drag it out. Thatch, or the milder accumulations known as 'mat', is most likely to become excessive where creeping grasses predominate and on soils that have become acid through excessive feeding.

Removing deep-seated debris or 'thatch' from a lawn in autumn with a spring-toothed rake. Lighter rakings should be given once a fortnight from spring to late summer.

Brushing with a besom or one of the modern lawn brushes has the same effect as raking but does not, of course, penetate so deeply. Brushing also disperses worm casts.

It is part of good lawn management to remove debris before it accumulates to this extent, and raking is the first step towards this. A spring-toothed rake should be used to avoid damaging the turf, and a light raking may be given once a fortnight from spring to late summer. Then in the autumn, before the autumn feed is applied, a much more severe raking may be given to drag out deep-seated debris. Raking also helps to eliminate clover and other creeping weeds and will remove some moss though it is seldom entirely effective in getting rid of it.

Brushing has much the same effect as raking, but does not penetrate so deeply. It is also necessary to disperse worm casts before they get trodden or rolled down and it will remove debris dragged out but left behind by the rake. The old-fashioned besom, made of birch twigs, is still an excellent lawn brush, though it is fast disappearing, its place being taken by specially designed lawn brushes.

Slitting

Slitting is a counterpart to raking and is sometimes referred to as 'vertical mowing' since it cuts the long horizontal threads of grass and roots which help to form the mat or thatch and bind it together, throwing much of it on to the surface where it can be removed with rake or brush.

All kinds of apparatus are available for slitting ranging from simple hand-propelled models to big power-driven machines and some for attachment to lawn mowers, but since the latter place a considerable drag upon the machine it is necessary to make certain that the mower is sufficiently strongly made and has a powerful enough engine to take the load. This is the crux of the whole matter since penetration, to a depth of at least 4 cm (1½ in), is essential if the slitting blades are to do much good, and with lightweight hand-propelled machines it may be difficult to get this penetration. Light slitting to a depth of 2.5 cm (1 in) may be done at any time in spring or summer, but once every autumn, fine quality lawns should be given a deeper slitting.

Lawns on heavier soils and those which are much used may need spiking to allow air and moisture to penetrate the soil. A foot-operated hollow-tiner takes out small cores of turf. These can make a valuable addition to the compost heap.

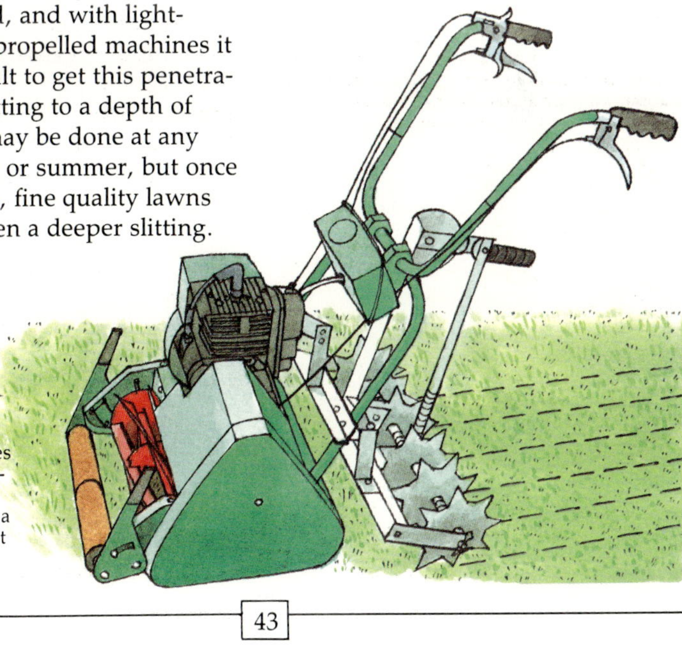

Slitting, sometimes referred to as 'vertical mowing' can be done by fixing a special attachment to a powered mower.

The simplest method of spiking a lawn is to use a garden fork. Drive the tines in about 8 cm (3 in).

Pull back on the fork to lift the turf a little. Repeat this operation every 10 cm (4 in) or so. This task will prove hard work on a lawn of any size and can be carried out in stages.

In September the grass should be thoroughly raked (see illustrations on page 42) and top-dressed with peat. If the surface is hard and compacted it should first be spiked, as shown on pages 43 and above.

The peat can be worked in quite easily with the back of a spring-toothed rake or with a besom or broom.

Aeration

Spiking and hollow-tining have a different purpose. They are intended to let air and moisture penetrate soil that has become compacted by too much use. On the home lawn they may not be necessary at all. Much depends on the type of soil and the amount of treading the lawn gets. Heavy clay soils are more likely to need spiking or hollow-tining than light sandy ones, and so are lawns frequently used for games.

Spiking at its simplest can be done with an ordinary fork thrust 5 to 8 cm (2 to 3 in) into the soil and then slightly pulled back to raise the turf a little. This is repeated every 10 to 15 cm (4 to 6 in) all over the lawn. It takes time, but is entirely effective.

Again manufacturers have been busy designing labour-saving machines and there are lawn spikers of all kinds, from small hand-propelled models to power-driven machines. So long as they give the necessary depth and frequency of perforation, choice can be determined by one's pocket.

Hollow-tining is simply a refinement of spiking. Instead of making a hole in the turf by pressure, the hollow-tined fork or machine removes a little plug of turf. This is really a better job and the real lawn enthusiast will probably prefer hollow-tining to spiking, but the differences are marginal and both can be effective if properly done.

The best time for spiking or hollow-tining is autumn and this may well be made a regular part of the early autumn programme when the lawn is given a thorough overhaul.

Maintaining the edges

Trimming the edges of a lawn has little to do with its health but everything to do with its appearance. Neatly cut edges look smart and the grass growing over the edges should be attended to every time the lawn is mown. For this purpose long-handled edging shears are excellent and are quite speedy to use, but even faster edge cutting can be done with one of the mechanical or electric edging tools available.

Constant mowing and even more rolling tend to make edges spread, and ordinary wear can have the same effect. In addition, soil from beds tends to settle against the

All lawn edges need cutting back periodically. A spade can be used for this purpose or, much better, a special half-moon edging knife. Always work against a long plank to obtain a really straight line when cutting.

Well cut lawn edges can greatly improve the appearance of gardens and this work can be done most quickly with an electrical tool. The lightweight edger (left) cuts with a nylon cord and is ideal for trimming around curved beds and into awkward corners, while the heavy duty model (right) cuts down work on the long edges around large lawns.

To keep a lawn looking neat the edges must be regularly trimmed; ideally every time the lawn is mown.

lawn edges. To correct these faults the edges must be cut back occasionally, either with a sharp spade or a special lawn edging knife. To ensure a straight cut either a line should be stretched between pegs to mark the true edge of the lawn, or a straight-edged plank should be laid and the cut made to this. If a fairly long nail is driven right through the plank at each end so that these spike down into the turf when the plank is laid flat, it will be held firmly in place while the cut is being made.

Opposite: The wide grass path curves to follow the lines of the beds and is, therefore, easy to mow.

To repair a lawn edge, first cut out a square of turf around the damaged area.

Ease the cut turf foward and trim a fresh edge flush with the rest of the lawn. Then seed the remaining patch of bare earth.

Two pieces of board can be used to enclose heaps of leaves to load them into a wheelbarrow.

Autumn leaves

Autumn leaves should not be allowed to lie on the lawn for long periods or the grass will suffer. A spring-toothed rake is a good tool for this job but a hay rake is better. For larger areas a mechanical leaf sweeper is useful. Some models can be pushed by hand, some towed behind ride-on lawn mowers and some are power operated.

On larger lawns a mechanical leaf sweeper can save much time and energy.

CHOOSING AND MAINTAINING A LAWN MOWER

Choice of grass cutting equipment must be determined partly by the type of lawn required, partly by its size and also by the amount of money that can be spent.

Types of lawn mower

There are three main types of cutting equipment available for lawns: cylinder or reel lawn mowers which give a scissors type cut between revolving blades and a fixed bottom blade; rotary grass cutters which slash the grass off with the action of a scythe or sickle, and flail grass cutters which also slash the grass off but with small hinged blades mounted on a rotating cylinder.

Cylinder lawn mowers differ in being driven by either wheels or rollers, in width, in the number of revolving blades on the cylinder, in the ratio of gearing between cylinder and wheel or roller and in being hand or motor-propelled. The last is merely a matter of convenience and has no bearing on the type of cut given to the lawn. This depends almost entirely on the number of blades on the cylinder and their gearing (see page 31).

Width for width, the more cuts a machine gives per metre, the more power it is likely to require to propel it forward. Again, this is to some degree dependent on good design, well-made bearings and proper oiling and good maintenance.

However, it is broadly true that a 40 cm (16 in) machine giving 100 cuts per metre is about as much as anyone would want to push by hand and a good deal more than most people would be prepared to tackle.

A high rate of cutting is a positive drawback if fairly long or wet grass is to be cut, as it will increase the liability of the blades to jam. Special rough-cut machines are made for this purpose. Lawns cut with these machines will inevitably have a slightly ribbed appearance, but they are quite suitable for the Continental type lawn, mown to about 2.5 cm (1 in). Most rough cut cylinder mowers throw the grass out backwards so that, if used without

The simplest type of lawn mower is the side-wheel cylinder or reel mower. Such machines have the advantage of being able to cut rougher grass than their more sophisticated roller-driven counterparts. However, they cannot cut up to the edge of the lawn.

The hover mower (below) is excellent for dealing with steep banks. Plastic blades (above) are available to fit a number of models. These are suitable for the frequent light mowings necessary during the summer months and are easy to fit.

Mains-powered electric mowers are restricted by the length of the cable.

pick-up box, the machine does not get cloggd up with the grass already cut.

Rotary machines will tackle long grass or short, but seldom give such a clean, even finish as cylinder machines. In this respect the finished effect depends partially on the good design of the machine and partially on keeping the revolving blades really sharp. They tend to wear down rather rapidly and may have to be touched up with a file every two or three weeks.

Rotary machines are always power driven, but in the majority of small- to medium-sized machines – 30 to 50 cm (12 to 20 in) width – the motor only drives the revolving blades and the machine must be pushed forward by hand. The more slowly it is pushed the cleaner the cut will be. However, there are some fully power-driven machines and these are to be preferred if a fairly large area of grass has to be dealt with at regular intervals.

There are not, as yet, a great many machines operating on the flail principle and they are all intended primarily for fairly large areas of grass. They are capable of dealing with very rough conditions but have not much use in ordinary gardens.

Side-wheel mowers are usually cheaper, size for size, than roller mowers and may take fractionally less energy to propel, but otherwise have not much advantage except for rough cutting. They cannot be operated over the edge of a lawn as a roller machine can, and so they leave the additional job of trimming the grass growing upwards at the edge. Moreover the roller mower

Where long and short grass has to be cut and a clean, completely even finish is not considered essential, a rotary mower is the answer. The model illustrated has a grass box but this feature is not always incorporated in the design. The wheel height is adjustable. Some models come fitted with a front roller to give the popular striped effect (inset).

does roll the grass lightly and leave the striped surface which most garden owners find attractive.

Either cylinder lawn mowers or rotary grass cutters may be powered by petrol engines or by electric motors. The petrol engines may be 2-stroke or 4-stroke and there is a preference for the latter because of supposed superiority in starting. However, modern 2-stroke engines are usually very reliable in this respect and are actually preferred by some because of their low maintenance cost and mechanical simplicity. Vertical engines are nearly always used for cylinder machines, but most small rotaries are powered by horizontally-mounted engines with a vertical shaft driving the rotating blades direct. This reduces mechanical complications to a minimum and reduces the costs.

Many rotary machines are available powered by electric motors obtaining their current by cable direct from a mains supply. Care must be taken to keep the cable away from the cutting blades.

A number of cylinder machines are electrically powered, some being offered in alternative models, petrol or electric, the latter drawing their current by cable direct from the mains supply.

Advantages of the electric machine are low running cost and maintenance, reliability, certainty of instant starting, whatever the weather, and quietness. The main drawback is dependence on a mains electric supply, the limitation in the area that can be covered because of the cable, and the necessity to keep this away from the blades.

Air-cushion mowers

Many rotary mowers have no wheels but ride on a cushion of air made by a fan attached to the shaft that drives the blades. Advantages are reduction in moving parts and the ability to be moved equally easily in all directions. These hover or air-cushion mowers can be slipped easily under overhanging branches of shrubs and can be used on steep banks either by standing on the top of the bank and swinging the mower like a pendulum or by lowering it down the bank on a rope. Some models are designed to pick up the cut grass.

A large, ride-on motor mower for cutting extensive grass areas. This machine provides a clean-cut sward of impressive evenness, if correctly maintained and adjusted.

Ride-on mowers

Many petrol engined mowers are designed with a seat to carry the operator and larger models are designed, like tractors, to use other tools or equipment beside grass cutters. Most of the small ride-on mowers use the rotary cutting principle but cylinder models are also available. All types can reduce the time and labour of cutting large lawns considerably and the larger rotary models can also tackle rough grass quite efficiently.

Safety

A great deal of attention has been paid to increasing the safety of all types of power driven lawn mowers. These include double switches for electric machines, clutch levers that immediately disconnect the clutch and stop the machine and/or blades if released by the hand, special insulation and much use of plastic instead of metal blades in some rotary mowers. Another development is the nylon cord cutter or strimmer which uses a short length of flexible nylon cord revolving at great speed to cut grass. If the cord hits a hard object it simply folds back doing no harm to itself or the obstruction and so strimmers can be used to cut grass growing against walls, fences and posts.

Maintaining a mower

Whether you have the latest model or an old petrol driven mower it must be properly maintained. Petrol engines must be correctly supplied with oil, and plugs must be kept clean and renewed periodically. The valves of 4-stroke engines will probably need grinding-in once a year and both 4-stroke and 2-stroke engines may need actual decarbonising.

All cylinder machines are likely to need regrinding once a year. This should be done by an expert on a special machine, otherwise there is danger of the blades being ground unevenly and not making correct contact throughout their length.

The blades of rotary machines can usually be sharpened quite easily at home on a grind-stone or with a file, but at the height of the cutting season they may require attention every two or three weeks. When they wear out they are readily replaced.

All cylinder machines have means for adjusting the pressure of the revolving blades on a fixed bottom blade, but since this differs from one make to another, manufacturers' instructions should be consulted. When correctly adjusted, the blades, when revolved slowly by hand, should be capable of cutting a sheet of notepaper at any point along their length.

All moving parts and bearings must be kept well oiled and in winter it is advisable to smear all cutting edges with oil or grease to prevent rust. Particular attention should be given to flexible cables controlling throttles, electric switches and clutches since these may rust internally and then stick or break unless regularly oiled.

Regular maintenance is essential if any mowing machine is to work efficiently over a long period. This means cleaning the exposed parts.

Oiling the driving chains, a vital part of the mechanism which must receive regular lubrication.

The blades should always be kept clean and sharp if a clean 'cut' is to be achieved. It is especially important to remove any traces of grass or mud which may have adhered to the blades after every cut.

Adjusting the driving chains which may become slack through constant use. This job is sometimes overlooked as the chain is out of sight behind its protective cover.

LABOUR SAVING

The most time-consuming task on all lawns is mowing and if labour is a serious consideration it is worth considering ways of reducing the time spent on this.

Lawn design

First there is the design of the lawn itself. If it is surrounded on all sides by cultivated ground, turning at the end of each cut becomes more difficult and it is probable that cross cutting at each end will be necessary to ensure a clean finish. But if space is left at each end of the lawn for turning so that the machine can be run right off the lawn, turned and a new cut started side by side with the last cut, time will be saved. If a path is used as the turning point it will need to be smooth and level with the lawn. Obviously for this purpose smooth flagstones or concrete are to be preferred to crazy paving or gravel.

Paths at the side of a lawn or cutting through it should be sunk about a centimetre below the level of the soil so that the blades of the mower can cut right up to the edge of the grass, with the mower partly over the edge of the path, without risk of damage to the blades. Raised paths, walls and rock gardens abutting lawns are time consuming since no ordinary lawn mower can be operated right up to them so that final cutting must either be with shears or nylon cord strimmers, or a clear cutting space must be maintained between lawn and obstacle, involving extra edge trimming.

If beds are cut out of lawns it will save time if they are of shapes that will permit cutting in the same broad lines as the lawn itself. Rectangular beds with sides parallel to those of the lawn are usually the easiest to negotiate. Large circles and ovals can be cut around without too much trouble, though they usually involve a few extra journeys with the lawn mower. Complex beds can double the cutting time for a lawn, besides presenting all sorts of problems in edge maintenance and this is something to take into consideration.

This true lute is one of the many modern labour-saving devices which can be used to apply a topdressing evenly and quickly.

Plants growing out on to lawns from adjacent beds or borders can damage the grass and make it very difficult to mow and to trim the edge. This can be overcome by laying a strip of paving slabs between the cultivated ground and the turf, so that the plants lie on the slabs. These should be laid 1 to 2.5 cm ($\frac{1}{2}$ to 1 in) below the lawn level and a gulley at least 5 cm (2 in) deep and wide left between the lawn and the slabs so that the grass does not grow out on to the slabs. Of course, the edge of this gulley will have to be trimmed, but since it simply replaces the edge which otherwise would have been with the cultivated ground, it does not represent any extra work. Incidentally, if the bottom of the gulley is carefully watered with simazine no weeds or grass will grow in it, but this weedkiller must not be put on the lawn itself.

Choice of lawn material

Before deciding what kind of lawn to make, it will be wise to consider how much time can conveniently be given to its maintenance. Broadly speaking the finer the grass the more care and mowing it will need. Where a bowling green may need almost daily cutting from May to September, a display lawn of rye-grass or meadow grass may be quite satisfactory with once-weekly cutting for most of this period. Moreover, such lawns can be very easily cut with rotary mowers which can be used in almost any weather and condition of grass, whereas the multi-bladed cylinder mower needed for the finest cutting can only be used when the grass is reasonably dry and short.

Correct equipment

Proper equipment will, of course, save a lot of time and labour. Even with hand-propelled lawn mowers it pays to buy the best, not only because of the better quality cutting such machines are likely to give, but also because they are easier to use and are more reliable. Long-handled shears will save time and back-ache in dealing with edges and awkward places and in large gardens a mechanical edge trimmer can save you hours of work.

It pays to have a proper lawn rake of ample size as this will do the work efficiently and quickly. Similarly if lawns are to be used a great deal, and therefore are likely to require frequent spiking or slitting to overcome compaction, it will save much time to purchase the correct mechanical equipment to do this. Aerating a lawn with a fork is a long and tedious task.

A good fertilizer distributor will not only apply lawn feeds more accurately and evenly than they can be put on by hand, but will also save time and mess. Moreover, if the lawn is fairly large it will pay to buy a wide distributor which will be almost as easy to push as a narrow one and will greatly reduce the time and walking required to cover the lawn.

Similar considerations apply to the purchase of lawn mowers except that here one must remember that extra width of cut does considerably increase the power needed to propel the machine. This also applies to the number of blades on the cylinder of reel-type machines and the number of cuts per metre that the machine will give. So when considering hand-propelled machines it may well be better to choose one that is 30 cm (12 in) wide, even though this will mean more journeys up and down the lawn, than to have a 35 cm (14 in) machine which will save time but require considerably more effort per metre.

Removal of lawn clippings

A considerable amount of time and effort is consumed in removing grass clippings from lawns. If the lawn is cut fairly frequently and the machine is of the type that scatters the clippings evenly they may be allowed to lie, at any rate in summer, when they wither quickly. However, some rotary grass cutters throw out the clippings in swathes which lie heavily on the grass and can kill it. So if the machine is not fitted with a collecting box, the clippings must be raked up afterwards, and this can take a considerable time. Small grass boxes must be emptied frequently, so it pays to buy a machine with a grass box of ample size. If the mowings have to be removed to a compost heap at some distance from the lawn it will also pay to invest in a large wheelbarrow or to have extension sides to a wheelbarrow so that it can take a good load. Grass mowings do not weigh much but are very bulky.

If there are rose beds or a shrub border around or near the lawn it may be possible to save a lot of time by discharging the lawn mowings straight on to these, spreading them evenly with a rake as soon as mowing is completed. Fresh lawn mowings make an excellent mulch which will retain soil moisture, feed the soil, smother small weeds and in some cases restrict diseases by preventing spores being blown or splashed from soil to plants. Good results have been reported in the control of rose black spot by maintaining a constant mulch of lawn mowings over the beds from April to September. However, fresh grass mowings should not be applied as mulches for two or three weeks after the use of selective weed-killers, though they can be placed on the compost heap provided this is not to be used for some months. Mowings are best scattered over harder material in the compost heap, when they will assist rotting. If placed in great thickness alone they make a rather sticky mess.

List of lawn grasses

Chewing's Fescue. A tufted grass with needle-like leaves, capable of producing the highest quality turf. One of the most popular ingredients of high quality lawn mixtures, but needs a more creeping grass as a companion to give good all-over cover.

Creeping Red Fescue. Similar to the last, but leaf slightly broader and plant more spreading in habit.

Sheep's Fescue. A fine needle-leafed tufted grass, but less tolerant of varying soil conditions than either Chewing's Fescue or Creeping Red Fescue.

Browntop. This is the species of agrostis or bent grass most commonly used in fine lawn mixtures, often in association with Chewing's Fescue. The leaves are narrow but not needle-like, and the best forms spread quite a lot so helping to form a well-covered sward.

Brown Bent. Not to be confused with Browntop. Very narrow leaves and creeping habit. Like the last it makes an excellent companion for the fine tufted fescues.

Velvet Bent. Very similar to the last in leaf but much more spreading in character. It produces a rather soft lawn which is springy to walk on.

Creeping Bent. A very variable plant, creeping in habit, roots near the surface, forms a thick springy turf and does not stand drought or close mowing. It can be grown from seed or from tufts.

Perennial Rye-grass. Strong-growing with comparatively broad leaves, it grows well in most soils, but does not stand really close mowing. The long seed stalks are tough and cannot be cut easily with cylinder lawn mowers. There are a number of different varieties specially bred to overcome these faults, give a dense turf which wears well and retains a good colour even in winter. Hunter and Elka are examples.

Smooth-stalked Meadow Grass. Strong growth and good colour, even in hot dry weather. The leaves are comparatively broad, and it does not like close mowing. There are selected varieties such as Benson and Primo.

Rough-stalked Meadow Grass. Similar to the last in appearance and able to survive under trees if the cover is not too dense. This is the usual ingredient of lawn mixtures for shady places.

Timothy. A strong-growing grass which wears well and will succeed on fairly heavy soil, but not suitable for very close cutting.

Crested Dog's Tail. A fairly broad-leaved grass which can be close mown, but produces wiry seed stems that sometimes defy a cylinder lawn mower. It will grow on poor or chalky soils.

SEASONAL GUIDE TO LAWN CARE

January

Preparation of sites for new lawns may be carried out when weather permits.

February

Lawns may be mown lightly when reasonably dry. The preparation of sites for new lawns can continue. Advantage should be taken of dry weather to break down clods.

March

Mowing should continue at slightly increased frequency. A roller may be used once when surface is not too wet. Under similar conditions lawns may be raked. Towards end of month apply a lawn fertilizer. If worms are troublesome apply chlordane or Mowrah Meal. Grass seed may be sown later this month and turf laid.

April

Gradually increase frequency of cutting and cut fine lawns rather more closely. This is usually a good month for sowing grass seed and also for laying turf. Apply spring fertilizer if not already given in March. This also applies to chlordane and Mowrah Meal for earthworms. Apply an insecticide if leatherjackets have proved troublesome. Apply weedkiller or mosskiller as necessary. Roll fine lawns once or twice. Apply fungicide where disease has been troublesome.

May

Mow frequently with mower set at lowest cutting height desired for lawn. Roll fine lawns occasionally. Water if weather remains dry for several days. Rake occasionally to remove debris. Apply lawn sand to any weeds that have resisted earlier treatment.

June

Mow regularly, but not so frequently nor quite so closely if the weather is hot and dry. Apply fertilizers as in spring, but at half to two thirds rate. Water freely in dry weather.

July

Mow and water as in June. Prepare sites for August or September sowing. Apply selective weedkiller or lawn sand to weedy patches only.

August

Mow and water as in June. Towards the end of the month sow grass seed to form new lawns.

September

Continue to mow regularly. Blades may be set a trifle closer to the ground. Thoroughly rake turf and if there is much dead grass and debris below the grass, use a slitting tool. If surface is too hard and compacted, spike or hollow-tine. Then apply sharp sand and fine peat and brush in. Apply autumn fertilizer. Complete sowing of new lawns. Apply fungicide if disease has been troublesome. Complete preparation of sites for turfing.

October

Keep lawn swept of fallen leaves. Gradually reduce frequency of mowing. Complete sowing of new lawns as early in the month as possible. Lay turves. Complete raking, spiking or hollow-tining. Apply chlordane or Mowrah Meal, as directed by the manufacturers, if there is a worm problem.

November

Keep lawns swept of fallen leaves. Little mowing required. Lay turves during suitable weather if this was not done earlier. Prepare sites for sowing or turfing in the spring.

December

Overhaul lawn mowers, grass cutters and other tools. Cut fine lawns once if weather permits. Continue preparation of new sites for spring sowing or turfing.

INDEX

Figures in italics refer to illustrations